ISBN 0-9716567-3-8

The Gizmo Tales: Working Dogs
Jeri Fink and Donna Paltrowitz
Book Web Publishing, Ltd.
www.bookwebpublishing.com

Book Cover Design by Jeremy Ryan

How To Order:
Single or bulk copies can be ordered from:
Book Web Publishing, Ltd.
PO Box 81
Bellmore, NY 11710
or online at:
www.bookwebpublishing.com

**Visit us online at www.bookwebpublishing.com or
www.gizmotales.com**

The Gizmo Tales:

Working Dogs

by Jeri Fink and Donna Paltrowitz

Book Web Publishing, Ltd.

Books By Kids For Kids

We believe that kids are the best-equipped people to talk about their lives, worlds, and interests. We publish books by kids for kids, incorporating young people's voices, experiences, insights, and ideas in everything we produce. Through schools across the country, we invite kids to participate in the writing, editing, designing, reviewing, and promoting of their own book. Participants write a personal dedication, help illustrate the book, and draw an author self-portrait. Please take a moment to read what the student authors say about their work.

Thanks for listening to the kids!

Jeri Fink and Donna Paltrowitz

Thank you for making this project possible!

Best Buy Children's Foundation
East End Arts Council
Meadow Drive PTA
American Express

The Gizmo Tales: Working Dogs

*is dedicated to the children and staff at
Meadow Drive School where
"Everybody is Somebody"
and
the dogs and handlers in this book who
generously donated their time, knowledge, and
experience to show how working dogs are such
an important part of all our lives.*

Special thanks to:

Dr. Walter C. Woolley, who provided the original spark.
Russell Fink, for his enthusiasm and commitment to Book Web.

Ellen Schwartz, for her superlative editing skills.
Darren Paltrowitz, for his novel approach to thinking and editing.
Gizmo, for being our favorite Labradoodle.
Greg Rossi, for joining The Gizmo Tales *team.*
Jeremy Ryan, for his amazing artistry and technical advice.
Richard Fink, for his unquestioning belief in our work.
Rob Ratner, Director of Fine and Performing Arts for his support.
Roberta "Bunny" Chapman, for her hard work and love of kids.
Stacey Becker, for sharing her knowledge of books and publishing.
Shari Paltrowitz, for being our number one "reader."

Borders Bookstore in Westbury, New York for welcoming
Meadow Drive School student authors.

To our husbands, Rick and Stuart, and the young people in our
lives, David, Russell, Ann, Meryl, Tony, Stacey, Greg, Adam,
Yvonne, Darren, and Shari who share the optimism and vision of
their generation.

To the special seniors in our lives, Larry Milman, Sylvia Gelernter,
Harvey and Edna Fink, Robin March, and Herbert Michelson, who
leaped generations to join us in The Gizmo Tales: Working Dogs.

To our families and friends who share in all of Gizmo's Tales.
Thanks for your support!

In loving memory of Gladys Milman, Joseph March, Ruth Roth,
Judy Becker, Dora Eisenstein, and Persis Burlingame.

Dedications from the Student-Authors

Alex Goncalves	To my family, my pet Rex, and Mrs. Beyrer.
Alexandra D'Esposito	To my mom, dad, and twin sister. I love you all!
Alexandria Sais	To my mom, dad, sisters Olivia and Erica, friends, and pets. I love you all.
Alyssa Trivigno	To everybody who helped me write the book and to all of my family.
Amy Steinmann	To my mom, dad, brothers Robert and John, sister Angela, best friend Emily. I love you all. Thank you to all the people who helped us make this book.
Angelica Campagnoli	To my family and my dogs Kaiser and Coki
Anthony Molina	To my mom, dad, my brother, my sister, and Mrs. Van Bell.
Azra Canovic	To my parents, my sister, and my brother.
Brad Carlin	To my family, and best friends, Zack, Bobby, Dan, Bryce.
Brian Murtha	To my dad, mom, brother Jimmy, and Mrs. K.
Carly Rome	To my family, friends, the dogs and handlers that make up this book, and my dogs Sandy and Cosmo.
Daniel Sullivan	To my teacher Mrs. Beyrer, and to the readers across America.
Elena Portillo	To my family, Mrs. Van Bell, Mrs. K., Mr. Tramonte, and my friends.
Erica Antonison	To my pet, my mom, my brother, and my sister.
Jack Farley	To my friends, family, and all the teachers at Meadow Drive.
Jake Colletti	To my mom and dad, the authors, and my sister Jenna.
Jessica Shi	To my family and friends who have always been there and supported me along the way. I love you guys!
Jimmy Bulva	To my mom, dad, grandma, grandpa, the rest of the family, and all the teachers I had.

John Caputo	To my mom, dad, sister and other family. I also love you all.
Julio Vigario	To my teachers, Mrs. Van Bell, Mrs. K., Mrs. A., Mrs. Bond, Mrs. Y, and my family, pets, and friends.
Kaleny Mateo	To my family, friends, and teachers Mrs. Beyrer and Ms. Laurino. I love you all.
Kelly Ng	To my mom and dad, my sisters Jennifer and Stefanie, my grandma, and my two dogs Angel and Tigger.
Krista Thomann	To my mom, dad, brother, family and friends. Thank you all for being there for me when I needed you.
Lacey Fater	To my family and my dogs T.J. and Beau. I love you all.
Lauren Siemann	To my family, friends, and pets because they have always been there for me.
Luke Escobar	To my family, especially my brother Michael, my grandparents, all my teachers, and Mrs. Kasny and Mrs. Bond.
Melissa Casale	To my family, friends, and my two dogs Molly and Chuckles!
Melissa D'Esposito	To my mom, dad, grandma, grandpa, nanny, poppy, and sister Alexandra.
Michael Iannelli	To the authors, the people who came in so we could write about them, Best Buy, and my family.
Michelle Chin	To my loving family and great friends.
Nate Williams	To Mr. Tramonte, my family, and my dog Beeb.
Nick Fiori	To my mom, dad, sisters Jillian and Jenelle, my dog Jesse, my cousin John, and all the fifth graders at Meadow Drive.
Philip Wacker	To my family, pets, and four friends Zack, Brad, Jake, Josh.
Robert Steinmann	To my friends, family, and all the teachers who have inspired me to read. Hello to all the soldiers over seas.

Sergio Duarte	To my brother Nelson.
Steven O'Connor	To my mom, dad, brother Nicholas, and my teachers.
Tracy Reardon	To my family, friends, to the writers Jeri Fink and Donna Paltrowitz for making this happen, and for all the wonderful teachers who taught me all I know.
Tom Ward	To my mom, dad, brother Jimmy, sister Manda, and teachers.
Vincent Ciuffo	To my mom, dad, brother Peter, sisters Antonia and Francesca.
Vincent Pawlowski	To my mom, dad, brother, sisters, grandmas, and friends.
Willy Keaveney	To my mom, dad, sister Rachel, and my friends.
Zachary Rachell	To my parents, brother, sister, best friend, and my teacher.

Ms. Allison Collis	I dedicate this book to the talented students of Meadow Drive School. May you always indulge in the freedom to create. Your creativity will take you far in this world.
Mrs. Annette Karlewicz	I dedicate this book to the Class of 2004 at Meadow Drive and to my amazing doberman, Xena!
Mr. Anthony Tramonte	Congratulations to the class of 2004. Your achievement is a stepping stone for a bright future.
Mrs. Ellen S. Kasny	To my family at home, and my family here at Meadow Drive who inspire me each day.

Mrs. Jacqueline Teemsma

To Meadow Drive, a school striving for high standards and excellence for its students. To the 5th grade students of Meadow Drive who were always a pleasure to work with.

Mrs. Leslie Van Bell

To my Fifth Grade Students -- you worked so hard on this project. I loved watching you work and grow as readers and writers. I am very proud of all of you.

Ms. Lois Nelson

To all of us who work, I dedicate this book . . . man, woman, child and dog.

Mrs. Patricia Parendo

To my budding technologists, may you always find just the right "keys" to open the doors to your minds and hearts :-)

Mrs. Mary Ann Sieber

Dear Fifth Grade, Thank you for allowing me the pleasure of participating in your book project. Your hard work and enthusiasm will take you on coutlesss journeys through life. Enjoy each and every one.

Mrs. Mary Hale

To the class of 2004- working with you was a pleasure. Your hard work has been rewarded.

Mrs. Virginia Beyrer

To the Class of 2004 at Meadow Drive School: Your hard work and skill in writing made this book possible. You enrich my life everyday.

Mrs. Patricia Molloy

To my daughter Kristen, whose sensitivity and kindness to all human beings and animals, fills my heart with love. To my Meadow children, teachers and staff who enrich my life and make Meadow Drive the most wonderful place to work.

Table of Contents

Illustration by Vincent Ciuffo

Illustration by Carly Rome

Introduction

Meet Gizmo!

Gizmo

Did you ever meet a Labradoodle? That's me, Gizmo. I am part Standard Poodle and part Labrador Retriever. I am the very best dog in the world. Just ask the kids.

← Gizmo

I was born on September 22, 2001, at Rutland Manor, in Victoria, Australia. It is a very special place. A lot of horses, Labradoodles, and people live and work there. My mom's name is Becky, and my dad's name is Maverick.

Mom and Dad are both Labradoodles, too.

Becky

Maverick

3

Here are my brothers and sisters.

Beverley Manners took good care of all of us. When I was nine weeks old, Beverley got me ready to meet my new family. She played lots of different airplane sounds for three weeks. Beverley wanted to

be sure that I wouldn't be afraid when I flew to my new home in New York.

I had to wait until I was twelve weeks old to ride on a real airplane. Beverley gave me a big hug goodbye. I gave her a big lick. I was ready to move to New York.

My plane trip took a long time. My new family

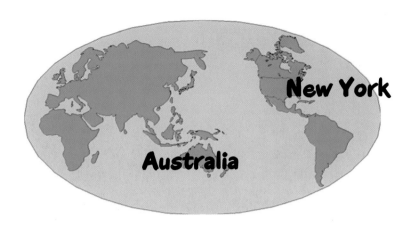

Australia

New York

was waiting for me at the airport. Everything looked different. There were so many new smells!

It was a short car ride to my home in Bellmore. Two crazy cats, Spock and Fiddles, lived in the house. There was still room for me. Now, I play with the cats, but my very best friends are dogs.

Birthday Party Arthur

Muddy Mimi

All Ears Clokey

My pal, Shari, always comes to play. She brings special toys and treats for me. She rubs my belly, too. Together we have so much fun.

I heard that a lot of dogs work every day. They have important jobs helping people.

I think I want a job, too. The kids at Meadow Drive School told me that there are many working dogs right here in the neighborhood. At their school we can meet some real working dogs. Maybe there is a special job for me.

Come join me and the kids to find out all about

working dogs. I'll even bring along the snacks, dog treats, of course. We'll have a lot of fun!

Illustration by Carly Rome

Part One

Gizmo & The Kids Meet Working Dogs In Their Neighborhood!

Gizmo and the kids meet
Sergeant Stephan Berger and Roo (Rooney)

Search and Rescue Dogs

by Angelica Campagnoli, Alexandra D'Esposito,
Alexandria Sais, Jessica Shi, Melissa Casale,
Nate Williams, Nick Fiori, Philip Wacker,
Sergio Duarte, Tom Ward

Illustration by Alexandria Sais

A search and rescue dog's job is to find people who are trapped, hurt, and lost so people like doctors and construction teams can rescue them.

Dogs can smell things much better than people. A trained dog can smell trapped people who are alive or dead long before a human can see them. Search and rescue dogs often find people by smelling a piece of their clothing. They can go into small places, buildings, and forests. If a robber is hiding, police can use their search and rescue dog to track down the criminal without using

a gun. The officer will command the dog to defend itself or stay cool.

A search and rescue dog has to have a lot of energy.

All About Roo

Roo is a great search and rescue dog. He has a lot of energy, experience, and loves to save people.

Roo is a German Shepherd, born on November 6, 1997. His real name is Rooney, but everyone calls him Roo. He was given to the New York City Police Department when he was ten months old.

Roo had to work very hard to become a search and rescue dog. He had to learn things like how to sniff a piece of clothing and find its owner, go into small places, and ride in helicopters, airplanes, and big moving machines.

Roo's most famous jobs were finding a kidnapped woman in Brooklyn and working at the September 11 World Trade Center terrorist attack. Roo found more than one hundred people in five years!

Now Roo is retired. He lives with the Berger family in their home. Sometimes Roo misses his job, but he has a big backyard and four kids to keep him busy!

Illustration by Melissa Casale

All About Sergeant Berger

Sergeant Stephan Berger is a very nice guy. We should be thankful for the many great things he has done in his very active life.

Sergeant Berger joined the Albertson, New York Volunteer Fire Department when he was a young man. Volunteer fire fighters don't get paid, so he took a job at the New York City Police Department at the same time. Later, he joined the K-9 Unit and worked there for seventeen years.

Steve has worked with three different search and rescue dogs in the New York City K-9 Unit. He found missing people, criminals, worked in collapsed buildings, and at the Oklahoma City and World Trade Center bombings. He is one of the many rescue workers in this picture taken

after the 9-11 World Trade Center terrorist attack. Steve and Roo retired from the Police Department in 2002. He is now Chief of the Albertson Fire

Illustration by Tom Ward

Department in Long Island, New York!

On September 11, 2001, twenty-three brave New York City Police Officers put the safety of others before themselves. They went to the burning towers of the World Trade Center to help their fellow New Yorkers. They did not return.

Sergeant Berger and Roo ask you to remember these heroes in your heart and prayers.

John Coughlin	Rodney Gillis
Michael Curtin	Jerome Dominguez
Walter Weaver	Ronald Kloepfer
Thomas Langone	Vincent Danz
Joseph Vigiano	Stephen Driscoll
Santos Valentin	Paul Talty
John Dallara	Timothy Roy
Claude Richards	Glen Pettit
Mark Ellis	Ramon Suarez
Brian McDonnell	James Leahy
John Perry	Robert Fazio
Moira Smith	

GIZMO'S COOL FACTS

- Search and rescue dogs are usually medium to large sporting breeds like Bloodhounds, German Shepherds, Golden Retrievers, and Labradors.
- Trailing dogs use the scent of a sock or glove to follow the path that a lost person has taken.
- Area search dogs are trained to find human scent in large areas. They can work off-leash.
- Water search dogs are trained to locate any human scent from under the water. These dogs work along the shore and in boats to find the scent as it rises through the water.
- Avalanche dogs locate people under the snow.
- Disaster dogs are trained to find people after earthquakes or buried under collapsed buildings.
- Search and rescue dogs were heroes after the September 11 terrorist attacks at the Pentagon and World Trade Center. More than 250 teams worked day and night to find people.

Illustration by Philip Wacker

13

Gizmo and the kids meet Nancy Allegretti and Zoie, Murphy, and Adeline

Therapy and Seizure Dogs

by Alyssa Trivigno, Brian Murtha, Carly Rome, Kristy Thomann, Lacey Fater, Lauren Siemann, Melissa D'Esposito, Michael Iannelli, Tracy Reardon, Zachary Rachell

Many people feel happy when they play with dogs. Therapy dogs are trained to work in hospitals, nursing homes, and schools. They cheer people up and make them feel better.

Therapy dogs are very gentle and friendly. They love to help people and are not afraid of loud noises, medical equipment, or machines. Therapy dogs can be any size, color, or breed.

Training is very important. The dogs take a test to show that they can obey commands like sit, wait, stay, and walk on a leash.

Therapy dogs work with people in wheelchairs, beds, and special homes. They even work with children in schools. The main job of a therapy dog is to make people feel happy. Some people think these special dogs work just like angels.

Illustration by Michael Iannelli

Zoie, Murphy, and Adeline

Nancy rescued three beautiful Golden Retrievers. She trained all of them to be therapy dogs.

 **Zoie** was once owned by very mean people. They kept her in a dark, scary basement tied to a rope. Zoie had no toys, bed, or food. Her fur and teeth were black from dirt. Nancy rescued her! Zoie was so skinny that you could see her bones. That's why Nancy calls her Zoie Bones.

 **Murphy** got into so much trouble that his owners did not want him. Nancy took him home to train. Murphy still did goofy things like eat feather pillows, walls, and real money. Now Murphy is big and heavy like a bear. He weighs one hundred pounds. That's why Nancy calls him Murphy Bear.

 **Adeline** was born in Europe. A family bought Adeline and shipped her to New York. Then they decided not to get a dog, so Nancy took her home instead. Adeline has pretty white fur. She eats as much as a pig. That's why Nancy calls her piglet.

Illustration by Carly Rome

All About Nancy Allegretti

Each week Nancy Allegretti dresses her dogs in special shirts. Then she drives them to Schneider Children's Hospital in New York. The shirts show everyone in the hospital that the dogs belong in the halls and rooms.

Nancy started a great dog therapy program more than eight years ago. She knew that many people felt better when they got a visit from a friendly dog. These days the dogs get into a line. They march in a parade up and down the halls. Lots of kids walk along with the dogs.

Illustration by Krista Thomann

Nancy loves to work with dogs. She was born in New York City. When she was growing up, Nancy always had dogs and horses. Now she has three therapy dogs. The dogs listen to her all the time. You can tell they really love her. Nancy Allegretti is a proud dog trainer and owner.

What is a Seizure Dog?

Sometimes a person may suddenly fall down, shake, or feel different. It is a medical problem that is called a seizure disorder. Something is wrong inside the body.

Children, adults, and even dogs can have a seizure

Illustration by Tracy Reardon

disorder. Nancy also has seizures. People with seizures go to school and work like everyone else. They must be more careful not to get hurt.

People usually do not know when a seizure will happen. Seizure dogs always know! They can smell the changes in a person's body. Their job is to make sure the person is safe.

Zoie is a therapy AND seizure dog. When she knows that Nancy will have a seizure, Zoie uses her paws to keep Nancy safe. Zoie knows that if Nancy is sitting down or on the floor, she will not fall and get hurt. Zoie, like all seizure dogs, is always right.

Nancy says, "I saved Zoie's life; then Zoie saved my life!"

GIZMO'S COOL FACTS

- Therapy dogs must experience things that do not usually happen at home. They must hear, see, smell, and even feel elevators, escalators, and all kinds of moving machines.
- Dogs are very sensitive to noises that people can barely hear. Therapy dogs must hear these sounds in motorized wheel chairs and respirators.
- Therapy dogs must be clean and healthy. They must allow strangers to groom them.
- Therapy dogs must be able to walk through crowds of people they don't know.
- Therapy dogs have to be calm when strangers and other dogs are nearby.
- When hearing loud noises, a therapy dog can't run away, be afraid, or show anger.
- Therapy dogs practice in restaurants when food is cooking, but not being eaten. They must know not to eat food left in hospital rooms.

Illustration by Lacey Fater

Gizmo and the kids meet
Billy Alemaghides and Meg

Geese Control Dogs

by Amy Steinmann, Anthony Molina, Elena Portillo, John Caputo, Julio Vigario, Kaleny Mateo, Vincent Ciuffo, William Keaveney

Many geese live in Canada. In the winter, Canada gets too cold for geese, so they fly south. The geese look for a warmer place with lots of grass to eat.

Geese fly to places like Long Island, New York, because there is a lot of grass and ponds. Geese like to live in the grass at parks, ponds, school yards, sports fields, and golf courses.

The geese create a very big problem. They leave droppings all over the fields. They pull out all the new grass that grows. The geese make such a big mess that people can't walk or play in places where a lot of geese hang out.

Long Island Geese Control is a company that makes geese fly away. There are special dogs that chase the geese away. Sometimes the geese hide in ponds. The dogs must be good swimmers to chase geese, but geese are much faster.

Illustration by Kaleny Mateo

Geese control dogs must run and swim fast to chase the geese. Making places safe and clean for people is an important job for dogs.

21

All About Meg

 Meg is a black and white Border Collie. She is very cute. She does not mind being around lots of geese and other dogs, but she is a bit nervous when she is with many people.

Meg was born seven years ago in the state of Massachussetts. Her owners did not want her. Billy paid $500 for Meg, and brought her home to Long Island, New York.

Meg is born to herd. It is her natural instinct or feeling to herd and chase geese. Meg never catches or hurts the geese; she just runs around them. She moves them into a group and makes them fly away.

It seems like a fun game to Meg, but she is really working. Billy gives her a pat on her head and a rub behind her ears for doing a good job. Meg and Billy make a great team because they help each other.

Illustration by Will Keaveney

All About Billy Alemaghides

Billy Alemaghides takes his dogs to work in the company truck. Long Island Geese Control is a company with many dogs.

The dogs travel by truck to parks, schools, sports fields, golf courses, and big lawns where geese are living. When Billy opens the truck doors, the dogs jump out and race to chase away the geese.

Billy's father started the business. At that time, Billy was a drummer touring the world in a rock band. In 1997, Billy went to work for his father.

There are now more people and fifteen dogs that work for Long Island Geese Control. These dogs, like Meg, live in kennels and love to work. In his free time, Billy still writes music and plays drums. He always liked dogs, and now takes them to work everyday.

Illustration by John Caputo

A Herding Dog's Job

A herding dog's job is to keep animals in a group and move them from one place to another. Herding dogs usually work with animals like cattle, horses, and sheep. Sometimes they are used for special jobs, like chasing geese.

Illustration by Vincent Ciuffo

The dogs run around the animals to keep them in a safe group. A good herding dog can give animals the "eye" so everyone knows who is boss!

Herding dogs keep animals safe in a pasture. They can also move them from field to field. Herding dogs sometimes guide other animals home. Farmers, ranchers, and shepherds have used herding dogs for thousands of years!

There are many different breeds of herding dogs, like Border Collies, Catahoula Leopard Dogs, Old English Sheepdogs, and Australian Cattle Dogs.

Illustration by Julio Vigario

GIZMO'S COOL FACTS

- Herding dogs control how other animals move.
- Herding dogs don't have to be tall. The Corgi, only one foot tall, can drive a herd of cows to pasture by leaping and nipping at their heels.
- Handlers use different ways to train their dogs. Words, sounds, signals, and whistles all command the dog to move in certain directions.
- There is a "tending" style of herding. The herding dogs act as a living fence to keep the sheep within the allowed grazing area.
- Herding dogs work quietly and calmly. They must be gentle, yet show strength when facing up to a stubborn animal.
- Real teamwork between the handler and herding dog is very important. However, herding dogs will think for themselves, if they believe that the handler has given a wrong signal.

Illustration by Amy Steinmann

Gizmo and the kids meet
Officer Terence Loughlin and Dan

Bomb Sniffing Dogs

by Amy Steinmann, Brian Murtha, Daniel Sullivan,
Erica Antonison, Kaleny Mateo, Kelly Ng,
Luke Escobar, Melissa Casale, Michelle Chin,
Steven O'Connor, Zachary Rachell

Bomb dogs have a great sense of smell. They are trained to sniff out bombs, dynamite, fireworks, and other dangerous things that can hurt people. These dogs find guns because they can smell even a tiny bit of gunpowder. Bomb dogs sniff mostly for explosives which are powders that can blow up.

Bomb dogs work in different places like airports, train stations, schools and sometimes parking lots. They go in elevators to check out skyscrapers where many people work. They also go to big events where there are a lot of people, like concerts and professional sports games.

Bomb dogs are trained to let the handler know when they smell danger. The handler calls the bomb squad so people don't get hurt, and buildings don't get damaged.

Illustration by Kelly Ng

All over the world bomb dogs are used because dogs smell a lot better than machines. These dogs make sure that places are safe for people.

All About Dan

Dan is a five year old German Shepherd. He was born in a country in Europe called Czechoslovakia. Dan came to the United States to work with his partner, Officer Terence Loughlin in the Nassau County Police Department.

Dan learned how to find many dangerous things. He practiced everyday to pass very hard tests.

Now Dan is a working bomb dog. He sniffs out bad things like bombs, gunpowder, and fireworks. When Dan finds something, he signals by sitting down. Officer Loughlin knows that there is trouble.

Dan also works as a K-9 Police Dog. He chases bad guys, finds lost people, and searches buildings. One day a man stole a car, crashed it at the mall, and ran away. Dan caught the thief! After the 9-11 attacks on the World Trade Center, Dan and Officer Loughlin spent many hours helping out.

Illustration by Erica Antonison

To stay strong and healthy, Dan eats only dog food. His favorite treat is getting to play with Officer Loughlin.

All About Officer Loughlin

For as long as he could remember, Terence Loughlin always wanted to be a policeman. He dreamed about it when he was a kid.

He made lots of good choices and passed many tests to get the perfect job. Now Officer Terence Loughlin works for the Nassau County Police Department K-9 Unit. His partner is Dan, a bomb dog.

When he was only a puppy, Terence chose Dan to train as a bomb dog. Dan had lots of energy and loved to play. Terence knew that Dan would use his energy to train and work hard.

When they are not working, Dan lives and plays with the whole Loughlin family. Officer Loughlin loves to ski and play basketball with his kids, too.

Illustration by Amy Steinmann

Terence and Dan stay together all the time. They must always be ready for an emergency. A call for help could come at any hour. If Terence gets a call, they rush to work. Terence and Dan make a great team!

A Police Dog's Job

There are many rules and laws to keep everyone

safe. K-9 dogs are trained to help make sure that people obey laws. K-9 dogs work in many different places. They work with people in the police department, the Air Force, and the Marines.

Illustration by Melissa Casale

K-9s must be strong, obedient, and very smart. They are trained to do many jobs that keep streets, towns, and cities safe. They learn to ride in cars, helicopters, trucks, boats, and chair lifts. K-9s find missing kids and lost adults. They also find bad guys so they can't hurt others.

Many K-9s have extra training in things like bomb sniffing and finding illegal drugs. They may spend hours learning how to do search and rescue work. Some K-9s, like Dan, do a lot of different jobs to help keep people safe. K-9s are part of hard-working teams that should always be treated with respect!

Illustration by Brian Murtha

GIZMO'S COOL FACTS

- They are called Bomb Dogs, Sniffer Dogs, Bomb Sniffing Dogs, Explosives Dogs, Detection Dogs, or Detector Dogs. Whatever name you choose, their purpose is to save lives.
- Bomb dogs train and practice from the time they are puppies. They are introduced to every kind of explosive and can find even the smallest amounts.
- Bomb dogs are used around the world. In the United States, they are used by police, the CIA, Special Service, and FBI.
- Teams search buildings, baggage, vehicles, open areas, airplanes, ships, trains, and stadiums.
- Bomb detector canine teams are tested to find different explosives. The handler is not told the amount or type of explosive they are searching for during the test.
- When they detect the scent of the explosives, bomb dogs must signal their owners before they reach the substance.

Illustration by Michelle Chin

31

Gizmo and the kids meet
Vinny Basile and Jesse

Guide Dogs

by Alex Goncalves, Azra Canovic, Brad
Carlin, Carly Rome, Elena Portillo, Jake
Colletti, James Bulva, Jack Farley, Kelly Ng,
Melissa Casale, Robert Steinmann,
Tracy Reardon, Vincent Pawlowski

Guide dogs have a very important job. They are the "eyes" for blind and visually impaired people.

Guide dogs must keep their handlers safe at all times. They have to find a clear path and stop at every curb. Guide dogs know when it is safe, and when it is not safe, to cross the street. If they make a mistake, it can be very dangerous for their handler. They are very smart!

Only puppies that are healthy, happy, and gentle become guide dogs. It costs a lot of money and time to train guide dogs to do their special jobs. A lot of dogs train, but only the best pass the final test.

Each guide dog is on a team with a blind or visually impaired person. The team lives and trains together. They become best friends.

Illustration by Tracy Reardon

33

All About Jesse

Jesse was born at the Guide Dog Foundation in Smithtown, New York. She is a pretty, small, black Labrador Retriever. When Jesse is wearing a harness, she is working. Her job is to keep Vinny safe at all times because he is blind.

Jesse takes very good care of Vinny. She leads him to the curb and waits for Vinny to listen to the traffic. Jesse pays careful attention to Vinny's commands. If he says "forward," Jesse will not go if it is unsafe to walk.

On airplanes, Jesse travels right next to Vinny. She even knows how to walk him safely on ice and snow. Jesse works hard to make sure Vinny does not trip or get hurt.

Jesse doesn't let people or other dogs take away her attention. She listens to Vinny all the time. Vinny trusts Jesse completely. She makes sure to lead the way for Vinny to get wherever he wants to go.

Illustration by Melissa Casale

All About Vinny

Vinny Basile is from a family of ten children. He was the youngest kid. When he was only five years old, Vinny became blind.

Vinny learned to use his ears instead of his eyes. He listened to everything. He heard the kids outside playing lots of games like jump rope, basketball, and baseball. He heard rhythms in the sounds that were all around him. Most of all, he loved to listen to the people who sang and made beautiful music.

When he was growing up, Vinny played a lot of music. Now he is a music

Illustration by Kelly Ng

teacher. Vinny also writes songs and plays in a band.

Vinny lives in Sea Cliff, New York. Jesse knows all about the house and the streets in town. Together, Vinny and Jesse go to work, shop, and walk to the deli. Vinny Basile thinks Jesse is a miracle. After all, Jesse gets Vinny everywhere safely!

Puppy Walker Families

Dogs, like kids, need to learn good manners when they are young. Puppies need lots of love and care.

Illustration by Robert Steinmann

Puppy walkers are people who make a puppy part of their family for just one year. The Guide Dog Foundation chooses these families very carefully. These very special families will teach the puppy to behave around lots of people and other animals. They will work hard to show the puppies all kinds of places. They give the puppies lots of love and attention so it will become a great Guide Dog.

A puppy walker family takes the puppy home at about seven to eight weeks old. They housebreak the puppy, teach it good manners and basic obedience. When the puppy is twelve to fourteen months old, the family brings the puppy back to the Guide Dog Foundation so it can be trained in its new job.

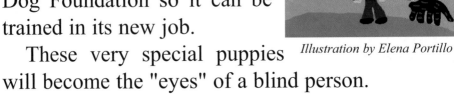

Illustration by Elena Portillo

These very special puppies will become the "eyes" of a blind person.

A Letter From Jesse's Puppy Walker Family

Dear Jesse,

Your foster mom was very sick, so I thought a puppy would help her. We got you from the Guide Dog Foundation and you loved us both right away! You could turn a bad day into a great day. You made your foster mom smile, something she had not done for months.

One day we went on a trip to Quebec. When we left home it was hot, but when we got to the cabin it was VERY cold. I turned on the heater. In the middle of the night you jumped on my head, barking. It seemed like a dream. You finally awoke me and my throat felt like it was on fire. I could hardly breathe! We had a hard time waking mom. She could hardly breathe, too. The heater had filled the cabin with bad fumes! I opened the windows and you sat next to us for the rest of the night. You saved our lives!

Now you will leave us and spend the rest of your life caring for someone very special. Mom and I will always love our Hero Dog Jesse and never ever forget you!

The Guide Dog Foundation

 The Guide Dog Foundation is in Smithtown, New York. Since 1946, the Foundation has given Guide Dogs to blind people for free! The Foundation wants to help blind and visually impaired people have a better life and be able to go wherever they want.

Guide dogs are born and trained at the Foundation. They have Labrador Retrievers, Golden Retrievers, and Labradoodles. Students come from all over the United States and the world to train with Foundation Guide Dogs. They also work with blind people who have hearing and walking problems.

The Foundation sends the dogs to Puppy Walker Families who give the puppies lots of love and attention. The puppies go back to the Foundation when they are one year old. For three to five months, they are trained to become Guide Dogs. Then a blind person and Guide Dog train together as a team for twenty-five days.

Illustration by Carly Rome

The Guide Dog Foundation spends more than $25,000 to train each Guide Dog!

GIZMO'S COOL FACTS

- When Guide Dogs wear a harness, they are working. Anyone who distracts the dog, can cause a dangerous problem for the dog and its handler.
- Always follow the rules below.
  1. Don't touch, talk, feed or distract the dog.
  2. Allow the dog to take care of its handler.
  3. Don't give the dog commands.
  4. Only the handler gives the orders.
  5. Don't walk on the dog's left side.
  6. Walk on the handler's right, a few steps back.
  7. Don't give the dog table food.
  8. Respect the handler's need for good dog habits.
  9. Don't let anyone tease the dog.
  10. Let the dog rest.
  11. Don't allow your pets or anyone to annoy the dog.
  12. Don't pat the dog on the head or play with him.
  13. Remember, a Guide Dog works really hard!

Illustration by Alex Goncalves

39

Wow! It's Gizmo again. I never knew there are so many working dogs in my neighborhood. The kids say that it takes special training to become a working dog. I would even have to do homework!

Julio says I need to decide if I have what it takes to be a working dog. It is not as easy as you think!

After all, it's great lying on the couch and eating dog treats. My life is fun playing with Shari and my dog friends Clokey, Arthur, and Mimi.

Am I the right dog for a job? Nate, Lacey, and Alexandra think I should ask the experts.

Part Two

Gizmo & The Kids Ask The Experts!

The Breeder:
Beverley Manners

Dogs are such wonderful creatures! They have feelings just like us. They can be scared, sad, happy, or excited. Some dog breeds have feelings that make them really good at certain jobs. Dogs work in a lot of different ways to help their human friends.

There are many kinds of working dogs. Sheep Dogs are bred to round up the sheep on big farms. Labradoodles are bred to be very special friends to people who need a "helping dog." Some dogs are bred and trained to be Guide Dogs and help blind people move around like everyone else. Other dogs are bred to visit sick people in the hospital, or to search for people who may be buried under a fallen building or lost in the snow.

The Sheep Dog feels happiest when he is running fast, like lightning, to head sheep in the direction his handler chooses. But he may not feel happy if he lives in a small yard as someone's pet. It is very important that each dog does the work to which his breed is best suited.

Illustration by Melissa Casale

The Veterinarian:
Dr. Paul LaPorta

The life of a working dog is very different than our pets. They work hard every day. Some of them work harder than adults!

A dog needs a lot of training to "work for a living." I help them along. All of our animal friends need good medical care, but our working dogs must be in "tip top" shape. Their eyes, ears, nose, and legs must work well so they can do their jobs. They do more than lay on the couch or play ball like the family dog. The working dog is the "eyes" for someone without sight, the "legs" for someone in a wheelchair, and the "nose" to find missing people. If they are healthy, they can do their job. If a dog is sick and can not make his weekly trip to the hospital, the kids will miss him. It will make it harder for the children to get well.

Our family pets love to please us. Working dogs are happy with their family AND their jobs, even if it makes them tired. We can learn about hard work from our furry friends. They are proud of what they do. They work hard every day. They never complain, and they love their jobs!

The Trainer:
Nancy Allegretti

There are many types of working dogs. They are chosen by their personality and how well they can do the job.

All working dogs learn basic commands like sit, lie down, stay, and come. The dogs' eagerness to do these simple things shows a trainer if it's the right dog for the job. It takes a special dog to be willing to learn all the lessons and still want to learn more!

When dogs have passed the basic commands, they go on for special training to learn their jobs. Companion dogs learn things like how to pick up objects, open and close doors, and turn on and off lights. Bomb and drug dogs learn how to sniff out things and tell the police when they find something bad. Search and rescue dogs learn to find people, whether they are lost in snow, the forest, or a fallen building. Therapy dogs learn to be gentle and kind with people in hospitals, nursing homes, and schools. Seizure dogs learn to tell their owners that a seizure is coming. None of this is possible until the dogs know all the basic commands.

*Illustration by
Vincent Pawlowski*

GIZMO'S COOL FACTS

WORKING DOGS

- Ricky the Rat Terrier is the smallest search and rescue dog in the U.S. He is seventeen inches high and weighs seventeen pounds. He squeezes into holes that other dogs and robots can't fit into.
- There are about 11,000 licensed working dogs. More than 4,000 are German Shepherds, 2,000 are Border Collies, 1,000 are Australian cattle dogs, and about 950 are Shetland Sheep dogs.
- People and animals give off scent particles. That's why dogs can track a scent through snow, air, mud, water, and even ashes.
- Dogs do not see fine details; they see moving things. They can see better at night than humans.
- Police K-9 Sirius was a bomb detection dog that searched hundreds of trucks and cars at The World Trade Center each day. He was the only police dog killed in the September 11 attacks.
- A natural gas pipeline was about to open in Ontario, Canada. Just in time, working dogs found 150 gas leaks forty feet underground.

Hi, Gizmo here! The experts tell me that I have what it takes to be a real working dog! The kids from Meadow Drive want me to find out a lot more about working dogs.

Vincent says all I have to do is go on the computer. I can meet a lot of working dogs all over the world. There are some crazy jobs for dogs.

Elena says says it's easy to find out about things

on the internet. I have to be smart and safe online. I'm going to do it. Just watch me!

I'm going to visit lots of different places on the computer. Come join me and the kids from Meadow Drive. We're going to meet some great working dogs online!

46

Part Three

Gizmo & The Kids Go Online To Meet Working Dogs Around The World!

Gizmo and the kids e-mail
Olivia de Travel Hound

Moss Vale, Australia

Olly: The Hot Air Balloon Dog

by Alex Goncalves, Kaleny Mateo, Kelly Ng

Olly is a three year old Labradoodle. Her full name is Olivia de Travel Hound. She was named after a beautiful movie star.

Olly was born in Rutland Manor, the same place as Gizmo. Now she lives with Suzanne Butz in Moss Vale, Australia.

Olly and Suzanne work on a hot air balloon named Penzance. They work mostly on weekends. Olly goes with Suzanne on very long trips. She helps people in the balloons when they are scared. Olly greets people and plays with the kids.

Hot air ballooning is Suzanne's main sport. Olly was only three months old when she started working. She was two years old when she started flying in the balloon. Olly and Suzanne like to go on many balloon adventures. They also like to compete.

Olly loves to make people laugh. Sometimes she dresses up as a pirate just for fun. People love to see a Labradoodle in clothes!

The E-Mail Interview

Kids: Why did you choose Olly as your dog?

Suzanne: I wanted a smart, fun dog who could do just about anything. I meet a lot of people in ballooning, so I needed a dog that was very friendly.

Kids: Does Olly ever get scared when she goes on the hot air balloon?

Kids: Hot air balloons can be scary. I use heat and flames to make the balloon rise. It makes a lot of noise. When Olly was little, I got her used to all the sounds. Olly had her first flight when she was two years old. She was not scared. She looked out over the edge as if to say, "Oh, so that's what the top of the trees look like." Olly is a very brave dog. When she doesn't fly, Olly is good at spotting my balloon and greeting us when we land.

Kids: What do you give Olly when she does a good job?

Suzanne: Olly gets lots of cuddles. Her biggest reward is to be able to play with people.

Meet The Authors

Alex Goncalves

Kaleny Mateo

Kelly Ng

Gizmo and the kids e-mail
KC and Andrea Mohr

Los Angeles, California

KC: The Dog Who Helps People

by Alyssa Trivigno, Erica Antonison, Sergio Duarte

Andrea Mohr likes to keep busy. Her kids went away to college and her husband worked many hours. She felt lonely and decided to get a dog who could help people. Andrea got a Labradoodle from Australia. She named him KC after the first letters of Kelowna, Canada, a place where Andrea and her husband love to visit.

KC is smart and easy to train. Andrea rewards him with dog treats and little pieces of hot dogs. KC always wears a bright red vest when he works.

Andrea and KC go to many places to help people. They visit the McBride School for kids who have problems. KC is gentle and patient. Some of the kids are scared because KC is big. After they get used to KC, the kids walk, brush, play, and cuddle with him. KC and Andrea also visit many hospitals and nursing homes. They work at Ronald McDonald House, where kids live with their families during medical treatment. KC has lots of fun giving big, juicy licks and kisses!

The E-Mail Interview

Kids: Does KC have other names?

Andrea: As KC grew up, and we got to know his personality, we gave him all sorts of nicknames like "The Doodle" and "KCDoodle."

Kids: Where does KC sleep?

Andrea: KC comes home at the end of the day and he is pretty tired. When he goes to bed at night, he sleeps beside my husband and me in his own bed. KC likes to sleep in. He is NOT an early riser. Sometimes I have to wake him up!

Kids: Do you have any special stories?

Andrea: Yes! KC has been asked to train for the canine crisis team with the Los Angeles Police Department. He will go to places where there has been a disaster and cheer people up. He will help take their minds off of their problems for a few minutes. Everyone always says that KC just makes them smile when he walks into a room, wagging his tail!

Meet The Authors

Alyssa Trivigno

Erica Antonison

Sergio Duarte

Gizmo and the kids e-mail Rudy

Riverview, Florida

Rudy: The Assistance Dog

by Jake Colletti, Julio Vigario, Lacey Fater, Tom Ward

Rudy is not even one year old, but he already has a job! Rudy is a miniature Labradoodle who was born in Australia. Brian and Kathie Scott brought him home when he was only nine weeks old. They named him "Rudy Dude" or "Rude Dude" after a sheep they owned when they lived in Ohio. Now Rudy lives in Florida with Brian, Kathie, and Lilly, a tiny Maltese dog.

Brian has a spinal cord injury and has trouble walking and picking up things. He needs Rudy to help. Rudy always stays close by. Once a week Rudy goes to school to learn to help Brian.

Rudy knows commands like sit, down, leave it, get it, come, wait, and stay. Rudy picks up things like pens, paper, watches, keys, and anything that drops on the floor. Rudy works on and off his leash. He can also open cabinets.

When he's not needed to work, he plays with his toys and Lilly. Rudy gets a lot of praise, pats on the head, and sometimes a treat for doing his job. Rudy is a very smart assistance dog.

The E-Mail Interview

Kids: Does Rudy like to work?

Kathie & Brian: One day I was folding towels from the dryer and dropped a washcloth. Rudy picked it up; I thanked him and gave him a treat. He then went in the bathroom, opened the cabinet with his nose, and brought me another washcloth so he would get another treat! I had no idea he knew where we kept them. He was so funny.

Kids: How did you start training Rudy?

Kathie & Brian: First, we would praise him "good boy" and say "thank you" when he would retrieve. Then we took a lightweight dog training dumbbell, put it in his mouth and said "take it." We held his mouth shut with the dumbbell in it and said "hold." Rudy learned not to drop things. We also taught him to "give," or "let go" of the dumbbell.

Kids: Can you tell any stories?

Kathie & Brian: One day Brian was having a rough time. He had to stay in his wheelchair. Rudy knew he was in bad shape, so he sat on the floor next to Brian and spent the whole day waiting and watching to see when he could help!

Meet The Authors

Jake Colletti

Julio Vigario

Lacey Fater

Tom Ward

Gizmo and the kids e-mail
Jim Cable and Bucca

Albany, New York

Bucca: The Arson Dog

by Amy Steinmann, Elena Portillo, Vincent Ciuffo

Bucca is a three year old Golden Retriever who was born in the state of Georgia. Bucca came to Albany to work as an arson dog for the New York State Office of Fire Prevention and Control Arson Bureau. Fire Investigator, Jim Cable, and Bucca work as a team to find how fires start.

A training program showed Bucca to find scents like gasoline, kerosene, and charcoal lighter fluid. These are liquids used to start fires. Bucca could sniff out even a tiny drop. At fire scenes, Bucca had to learn how to show Jim where these smells were strongest. By putting his nose on the spot and then sitting down, Bucca learned to signal Jim.

To train him, Jim rewarded Bucca whenever he found the right scent. The reward was Bucca's favorite toy, a rolled up white towel to play tug of war!

The team has worked hard at almost 500 fire searches. Bucca loves to work, which is just another one of his many favorite games.

The E-Mail Interview

Kids: Where did Bucca get his name?

Jim: Bucca is named in memory of Ronald Bucca, a Fire Marshal with the New York City Fire Department. He responded to the World Trade Center attacks on September 11, 2001, and gave his life in the line of duty. A New York City Fire Marshal investigates fires. I thought it would be great to name Bucca, who also investigates fires, in honor of Fire Marshal Ronald Bucca.

Fire Marshal Ronald Bucca

Kids: Where does Bucca live?

Jim: Bucca, who I sometimes call "Boo" or "Buc," lives at home with me, my wife, Lynne, baby Katy, Lucy, a Shih Tzu, and Wilma, our cat. When Bucca is home, he is just another member of the family. Bucca and Lucy are great friends. They spend time together chasing toys and snowballs.

Kids: Where does Bucca sleep?

Jim: Bucca has dog beds at home, in our work van, and at the office. When I go to work, Bucca has his own spot in the office, along with arson dogs Mica, Emma, and Alex who work nearby.

Meet The Authors

Amy Steinmann

Elena Portillo

Vincent Ciuffo

Gizmo and the kids e-mail Bandit

Brooklyn, New York

Bandit: The Resident Dog

by Azra Canovic, Daniel Sullivan, Michelle Chin

In 1998, Bandit was born to be a racing Greyhound. He was trained to race when he was a year old. He worked very hard, but his owners did not love him. Once Bandit got hurt and no one cared. They just wanted him to race and make money. When Bandit could not race anymore, his owners got rid of him for a new puppy.

Long Island Greyhound Transfer rescued Bandit and gave him to Irene Carr, Head of Special Projects at New York Congregational Nursing Center. It is a home for people who need medical help every day.

Irene makes it a very special place. Lulu the cat, birds, and fish live there. Everyone wanted a Greyhound, so now Bandit is their resident dog.

At first, Bandit limped because his leg hurt him. The vet took care of his old racing injury, and Bandit has no more pain. He loves to run outside and chase squirrels. Sometimes he runs from the dining room with bread in his mouth. The people at the center love Bandit. They help take care of him and Bandit cheers them up!

The E-Mail Interview

Kids: Why did you choose a Greyhound as a resident dog?

Irene: Greyhounds are not very active dogs. They are social dogs with very special personalities. Bandit loves to be with people. He is a gentle giant who is a couch potato. When sleeping, he curls up into his designer comforter. Greyhounds adapt well to their surroundings. Bandit was cat tested and he and Lulu get along well! Everyone here watches over Bandit.

Kids: Does Bandit have a special place to sleep?

Irene: Bandit sleeps in his own space at night. His food and comforter are with him. During the day, Bandit naps wherever people are. He suns himself in the community room. Sometimes he takes a nap in the small, cat bed by curling into a little ball!

Kids: Does Bandit have a nickname?

Irene: I call him Bandy or Baby Boy. He is such a good dog! He brings a smile to every face here.

Meet The Authors

Azra Canovic

Daniel Sullivan

Michelle Chin

Gizmo and the kids e-mail
Raquel, Razzberrie, and Ashley (reading)

Freeport, New York

Razzberrie: A Dog Who Listens To Kids Read

by Brad Carlin, Lauren Siemann, Melissa D'Esposito

Raquel Kliman was always scared of dogs. Then her husband, Steven, gave her a Keeshound puppy named Shamas. Raquel brought the puppy everywhere. She took good care of Shamas.

Soon Raquel loved having a dog. She was so happy when Shamas became the father of nine puppies! All of the puppies were born in Raquel's house. One of puppies is Razzberrie. Her nickname is Razzie from the color of her raspberry collar. When Razzie was old enough, a trainer showed Raquel how to teach Razzie to sit, stay, come, and give kisses.

Raquel and Razzie joined a group called Reading to Dogs at the Bide-A-Wee Animal Shelter in New York. Razzie loves kids and listens carefully to the sound of their voices. Razzberrie is often called the reading dog. She doesn't really read, she just listens. Kids read books about animals and explain words to Razzie. Her job is to help kids to read better by listening to every word!

The E-Mail Interview

Kids: What kind of dog is Razzberrie?

Raquel: Razzie is a Keeshound, a northern breed that comes from the Netherlands. They are the national dog of Holland. Long ago, they were called Dutch Barge Dogs because they lived on boats that traveled the canals. They would alert the Barge Master when another boat was coming. They also kept the children from falling overboard.

Kids: What is Bide-A-Wee?

Raquel: Bide-A-Wee has three great animal shelters in New York. It takes care of homeless cats and dogs until they are adopted. In one hundred years, Bide-A-Wee has helped one million animals find homes! Bide-A-Wee has a program called Reading To Dogs that helps children to read better.

Kids: How does Razzie read with kids?

Raquel: Razzie helps the kids read by listening. If she does not understand a word or idea, Razzie taps me with her paw. She "whispers" in my ear what to ask the child who is reading. Kids want to explain things to Razzie. She also helps children relax. Razzie and the kids have lots of fun reading together.

70

Meet The Authors

Brad Carlin

Lauren Siemann

Melissa D'Esposito

Gizmo and the kids e-mail
Deanna and Zippo

Carle Place, New York

Zippo: The Service Dog

by Angelica Campagnoli, Robert Steinmann, Zachary Rachell

Deanna McDermott is a very special teenager who lives in Carle Place, New York. She uses a wheelchair because she can't walk. Deanna has a back problem called Spina Bifida.

Deanna went to Dobbs Ferry, New York where she spent two weeks learning how to work with a dog. She was matched with Zippo, a service dog. Zippo was named and trained before she got him. He is a Golden Retriever, born on April Fool's Day, 1998. Deanna knew that Zippo was the right match for her. He brings her things that she needs all the time. Zippo loves the snow, just like Deanna.

Deanna loves wheelchair racing. Now she races every June in the Empire State Games for the Physically Challenged. She uses her wheelchair to play sports like tennis and basketball. For many years Deanna has been playing on a junior wheelchair basketball team. She stays in hotels and travels to all of her games along with Zippo. They make a perfect team, taking care of each other.

The E-Mail Interview

Kids: Do you have a favorite sport?

Deanna: For years, I've been on a junior wheelchair basketball team. The name of my team is the Long Island Lightning; my number is 12. We travel around the United States playing in different places like Pennsylvania, Michigan, North Carolina, Maryland, Alabama, and New Jersey.

Kids: What is Zippo like at home?

Deanna: Our house looks like we have a little kid because Zippo has so many toys. He loves little dolls and carries them around all the time. Tennis balls are his favorite. He always wants me to throw them to him. I taught Zippo to bring me his water dish when he wants water.

Kids: Does Zippo travel with you and your team?

Deanna: Zippo travels to all my basketball games. One day when everyone was cheering, Zippo let out a loud bark. Everyone started laughing. They said he was cheering, too!

Meet The Authors

Angelica Campagnoli

Robert Steinmann

Zachary Rachell

Gizmo and the kids e-mail
Lisa and Dude

Melbourne, Australia

Dude: The Companion Dog

by Alexandria Sais, Jack Farley, Nate Williams

The Madge family is from Melbourne, Australia. The parents, Wayne and Lisa, have two daughters, Kalynda and Natasha. They had a Labradoodle from Rutland Manor named Chloe, before Dude came to live with them.

Lisa has been ill for a long time. She has a rare disease that can not be cured. Friends and family are very sad. Even Chloe is unhappy and lonely.

At Rutland Manor, Beverley heard the sad news. She sent a Labradoodle, Dude, to cheer up Chloe, Kalynda, Natasha, and Wayne. When Dude arrived, he sensed that Lisa was sick and made himself her companion. Dude found Lisa's bedroom and quietly stayed next to her.

When Lisa went to live in a hospital, Dude cried at her bedroom door for four days. Finally, Wayne took Dude to the hospital. As soon as the elevator stopped, Dude pulled away from Wayne. He found Lisa's room all by himself. He jumped into Lisa's bed and gave her lots of doggie kisses!

The E-Mail Interview

Kids: Where did Dude get his name?

Wayne: He came from Rutland Manor named Cool Dude. We call him Dude.

Kids: How did Dude become a companion dog?

Wayne: Dude formed a connection with Lisa. He only wanted to be with her. One night he even let himself in through a window just to lie in the bed and cuddle with her. When he was put outside, he would stand at our glass door. If Dude saw Lisa being wheeled by in her chair, he would go nuts. Dude would hit the glass with all his weight. No matter what I tried, I could not stop him. Dude had to be at her side! It touched my heart.

Kids: Does Dude always stay or work at home?

Wayne: Dude came to see Lisa in the hospital. Although she had not spoken in two months, Lisa tried to say his name. Dude snuggled with Lisa for about two hours. Then I walked Dude around the hospital. Soon Dude had his own fan club. He went from room to room and was calm and loving to everyone.

78

Meet The Authors

Alexandria Sais

Jack Farley

Nate Williams

Gizmo and the kids e-mail
Dr. Janice Justice and Cajun

Portland, Oregon

Cajun: The Hearing Dog

by Alexandra D'Esposito, Jessica Shi, Philip Wacker

Janice Justice was a doctor and a teacher before she suddenly lost her hearing. A group called Dogs For the Deaf rescued Cajun from an animal shelter. They trained Cajun to be a hearing dog and gave him to Janice.

Cajun is Janice's ears. Smoke detectors or ringing phones are important sounds. When someone knocks on the door or calls her name, Cajun lets Janice know. He races to the sound and touches her leg. This leads Janice to the sound.

Sometimes Cajun hears things that are not as important. There could be a car outside or a cat meowing. Someone may walk into the room. Cajun will look in the direction of the sound. Then Janice knows to look in that direction, too.

Because Cajun must alert Janice during the night, he even gets to sleep on her bed. They go to school, work, restaurants, libraries, and on airplanes. Cajun and Janice are happy to go everywhere.

The E-Mail Interview

Kids: How did Cajun learn to sing?

Janice: I have a deaf friend, Guy, who taught Cajun to make little singing sounds. Soon Cajun was making all sorts of different singing sounds . He loved to sing and howl. When a singing contest came to Portland, Oregon, I entered Cajun. He won a trip to New York City. Cajun was chosen from hundreds of dogs to perform at Lincoln Center. He won second place! I was so proud of him.

Kids: What is Dogs For The Deaf?

Janice: Dogs For The Deaf is a group in Central Point, Oregon. Since 1977, it has trained more than 700 hearing dogs. The group rescues dogs from shelters and trains them. It takes about six months to train a hearing dog. The dogs must be alert, smart, and train easily. Once trained, the dogs are given to deaf people who need a helper. The dog and handler must learn how to work together as a team, taking care of each other.

Meet The Authors

Alexandra D'Esposito

Jessica Shi

Philip Wacker

Gizmo and the kids e-mail
Dudley Do Right

Boston, Massachusetts

Dudley Do Right: A Dog Who Makes People Smile

by Brian Murtha, Tracy Reardon, Steven O'Connor, Vincent Pawlowski

Dudley Do Right is a big, seventy-five pound Labradoodle who works with Leslie Kagan. They live in Boston, Massachusetts. One of Dudley's jobs is to welcome people who come to Leslie's office. Dudley greets them with a special gift. It's usually an old shoe or sneaker, but it makes people smile.

Leslie and Dudley also work for Caring Canines. They visit many different places. At The Home For Little Wanderers, Dudley does tricks for the boys. Then he runs outside in the backyard to play tag, fetch, and hide-and-seek with the kids. Dudley and Leslie also greet older people in nursing homes.

Kids love to see Dudley at the Children's Hospital Dog Show. Sometimes he dresses up like the wizard in Harry Potter, as a cow, or as G.I. Joe.

Dudley loves working with people. He has licks and kisses for everyone who asks. There are always lots of smiles when Dudley is around.

The E-Mail Interview

Kids: Does Dudley Do Right have a nickname?

Leslie: That's a long name, so I just call him Dudley. I also gave him some very silly nicknames like Doodleface, the Dudster, Duddles, Moose, and Fur-face.

Kids: How was Dudley trained?

Leslie: Dudley began puppy kindergarten two weeks after he came from Australia. He went to school for almost ten months. Luckily for Dudley, there wasn't too much homework.

Kids: What does Dudley like to do when he isn't at work?

Leslie: Dudley likes to watch for our mail carrier. She always brings him biscuits. He would love to deliver mail with her and eat biscuits along the way! Dudley's mail comes to his own e-mail address.

Dudley also likes to sleep, go for walks, and play with his sister in the garden. Dudley just got a new playmate to live with us from Australia. Her name is Gabby, and she's really Dudley's sister.

Meet The Authors

Brian Murtha

Tracy Reardon

Steven O'Connor

Vincent Pawlowski

Gizmo and the kids e-mail
Linda McKay and Kitty

Canton, Texas

Linda McKay: Cattle Dogs

by Carly Rome, Michael Iannelli, William Keaveney

Linda McKay thinks that Catahoula Leopards are the best dogs. She should know. Linda lives in Texas and owns thirteen of them. Catahoula Leopard Dogs live on farms and ranches where there is a lot of land. They work to herd or round up cattle, hogs, and horses. They are a very old breed, used by Native American Indians and early settlers.

Linda starts training her dogs when they are puppies. The puppies also learn by watching the older dogs. Catahoulas learn commands, hand signals, whistles, and words. They know things like "find a cow," "get out," and "get behind." When Linda points, her dogs know to turn right or left. They also know to STOP working when the cattle go into corrals or trailers.

Catahoula Leopard Dogs learn quickly and want to please their owners. They also love and protect the human family who they live with. Linda rewards her dogs by saying "good dog" in a happy voice and petting them. Catahoula Leopards are hard working dogs.

The E-Mail Interview

Kids: Why are Catahoulas good at herding cattle?

Linda: Catahoulas work on instinct; they think for themselves. They only need to be controlled and taught a few commands to herd cattle.

Kids: How do you reward them?

Linda: I call them to me, and give them a pat and say "Goooooooooooood dog!" They understand. They wiggle all over and bounce around, because it makes them happy to know they have done a good job. They try very hard to do what I ask.

Kids: Have you liked dogs all of your life?

Linda: Oh, yes! I've always been able to train and communicate well with horses and dogs. When animals know you like them, they will like you. Animals think differently than we do. When you're around animals, you should think positive, quiet thoughts and move very slowly. Never reach out suddenly towards an animal's head or grab at them. Touch them very slowly and gently, or they will be  frightened. If animals become afraid, they will bite, kick, charge, or run away.

Meet The Authors

Carly Rome

Michael Iannelli

Willy Keaveney

Gizmo and the kids e-mail
Ellen Graff and Jett *

*Ellen's retired racing Greyhounds are from New Hampshire
(Jett, Mocha, Chip) and Florida (Copperfield and Eddie)

Rosyln Heights, New York

Ellen Graff: Retired Racing Greyhounds

by Anthony Molina, Luke Escobar, Melissa Casale

Ellen Graff adopted five retired racing Greyhounds, Jett, Mocha, Chip, Copperfield, and Eddie because their owners did not want them. Long Island Greyhound Transfer, called L.I.G.H.T., is the New York group that rescued Ellen's Greyhounds.

Racing Greyhounds live a very hard life. They start training at twelve to fourteen months old. First the dogs learn at a training track. At eighteen months old, they start real racing. The dogs race from two years to five years.

There are 47 racetracks in the United States. Each year, owners retire or get rid of dogs who no longer win money. There are thousands of unwanted Greyhounds.

Ellen Graff now works for L.I.G.H.T. The group has saved over 700 retired, racing Greyhounds and found them good homes.

Racing Greyhounds are gentle, loving dogs. Ellen is doing a very important job by rescuing dogs and giving families wonderful pets.

The E-Mail Interview

Kids: How do you choose the dogs you want to rescue?

Ellen: Before there were groups like L.I.G.H.T., people would go to the track to get a Greyhound. You just took any dog they handed you, without any testing. You can imagine how many problems that started. Each dog is different, and each home is different. There had to be a system to match a dog to a home so everything would go smoothly.

Kids: Where do people find out about Greyhound rescue groups?

Ellen: The internet is loaded with Greyhound rescue sites. There are more than 200 adoption groups located in each state. These groups tell you what dogs are available and how to adopt them.

They will also tell you which racing tracks the dogs come from.

Kids: What happens to Greyhounds who aren't rescued?

Ellen: The dogs are "thrown away," often in a very mean way. Sadly, about 25,000 Greyhounds are put to sleep each year.

Meet The Authors

Anthony Molina

Luke Escobar

Melissa Casale

Gizmo and the kids e-mail Eilu and Yoki at The Wind River Bear Institute

Heber City, Utah

Lynne Rankin: Bear Dogs

by James Bulva, John Caputo, Krista Thomann, Nick Fiori

Bears eat a lot. They go to people's homes for fast and easy meals. Bears find food in fruit trees, garbage cans, dog dishes, and bird feeders. Sometimes bears destroy houses and barns when they look for food. They may even hurt people. To protect their homes, family, and pets, people may shoot and kill bears.

Too many bears were getting killed. Carrie Hunt wanted it to stop. She wanted the bears to get their food in the wild, not from people. Carrie started the Wind River Bear Institute to train special dogs called Karelian Bear Dogs (KBDs). The job of a KBD is to make the bears stay far away from people. That way, everyone is alive, safe, and happy.

Carrie has seven KBDs. The boys are Tuffy, Blaze, Yoki, Cassidy, and Satchmo. The girls are Eilu and Carmen. Eilu has eight puppies who will be tested to work with bears. People don't have to be scared of bears when there is a trained KBD around!

The E-Mail Interview

Wind River Bear Institute
"Partners-In-Life" Program: Working to Save Wild Bears

"Teach Your Bears Well"

Kids: What do you do at the Wind River Bear Institute?

Lynne: I'm a manager.

Kids: How are the dogs chosen for training?

Lynne: Carrie tests the KBD puppies at eight weeks. She takes them to visit a tame bear. The bear is eight feet tall, and the puppies are only eight inches tall! Some of the puppies look at the bear and run. Others stand and bark. Puppies who fearlessly take off after the bear are chosen for training. They will teach bears to stay away from people. We spend hundreds of hours training each dog. The other puppies are sold to families who want a nice dog, not a trained bear dog.

The bear's name is Tank, and he lives here in Heber City. He is very gentle, but the puppies don't know that. Tank starred in the movie *Dr. Doolittle* and on the television show *Growing Up Grizzly*.

Kids: What is the Partners In Life Program?

Lynne: We teach school kids in the U.S. and Japan about how important it is to keep bears alive in the wild, and people safe in their homes. KBDs help to make a peaceful partnership.

Meet The Authors

James Bulva

John Caputo

Krista Thomann

Nick Fiori

100

Part Four

The Kids Help Gizmo Choose His Job!

The kids and I found working dogs in the neighborhood and around the world. Dogs train and work hard to help people everywhere. Now it is time to find a job that's right for me.

Philip says that police dogs are cool. They work hard and help keep people safe. He loves search and rescue dogs like Roo.

Tracy likes therapy dogs. She thinks dogs like Zoie, Murphy, and Addy are very special because they make a lot of people happy.

Willy thinks that service dogs have the most important jobs. They help blind, deaf, and disabled people have a good life.

Philip, Tracy, and Willy are all right! Dogs are very special critters!

Which job should I choose?

I don't know what to do! The kids from Meadow Drive say that I should think of what I do best. Now, let me think of my favorite things.

I like to work with kids and learn about cool facts. I love to go to school, eat used bubblegum, and share gooey gummy worms. It is great sniffing smelly gym socks and digging in backpacks! There is nothing better than working with kids on computers.

Kids read and write all about ME. They send me e-mails and drawings, too. Everyone thinks I am a lot of fun. The kids think I can help people read and write books. Then everyone will have the chance to read lots of Gizmo Tales!

American Express

Best Buy Children's Foundation

Borders Books

East End Arts Council

Guide Dog Foundation

Long Island Nightly News

Meadow Drive PTA

Mineola Union Free School District

News 12 TV

Newsday

Part Five

People & Places Make It Happen

Special Websites

American Express
www.americanexpress.com
Best Buy
www.bestbuy.com
Bide-A-Wee
www.bideawee.org/
Book Web Publishing, Ltd.
www.bookwebpublishing.com
Catahoula Leopard Dogs
www.catahoulaleopard.com
Dogs For The Deaf
www.dogsforthedeaf.org
East End Arts Council
http://eastendarts.org
Guide Dog Foundation
www.guidedog.org
Kagan Associates
kaganassoc.com
LI Geese Control
www.ligeesecontrol.com

Long Island Greyhound Transfer (L.I.G.H.T.)
www.ligreyhound.org
News 12
www.news12.com

Newsday
www.newsday.com
NY State: Fire Safety for Kids
http://dos.state.ny.us/kidsroom/firesafe/
firesafe.html dos.state.ny.us
Olivia de Travel Hound
http://helpisit.com.au/labradoodle/
Rutland Manor
www.rutlandmanor.com
The Gizmo Tales
www.gizmotales.com
Therapy Dogs International
http://www.tdi-dog.org/
Wind River Bear Institute
www.beardogs.org

Part Six

Thanks!

From Dr. Lorenzo Licopoli, Superintendent of Schools

Congratulations on the publication of *The Gizmo Tales: Working Dogs!* The book is most interesting, particularly Gizmo -- the Labradoodle dog! I never knew about a dog like Gizmo who came to Long Island from Australia -- which is really far away!

The stories in your book were just great. It was terrific to meet all of Gizmo's friends and to learn about the many services that dogs provide for us human beings! Yes, indeed, I know I have learned a lot about dogs from your book. Thank you so much for working so hard. I know your community, school, parents and fellow students are proud of your efforts. Again, my congratulations to you and your teachers for a job well done!

Dr. Licopoli
by Philip Wacker

Dr. Lorenzo Licopoli
Superintendent of Schools
Mineola Union Free School District

From Mrs. Sherri Goffman, Director of Elementary Education

Dear Fifth Graders:

Congratulations on completing *The Gizmo Tales: Working Dogs* book! I realize that a lot of time, effort, and hard work went into researching and writing a book of this magnitude, resulting in an adventurous story that children and adults will enjoy reading. In writing this book you have also learned a great deal about dogs, writing, and working together as a team in order to achieve a common goal. As accomplished authors you have brought much pride to yourselves, your families, your teachers, and the entire Mineola School District. Thank you for sharing this very special story about Gizmo, the number one book on my summer reading list! Thanks for including me in this project.

Mrs. Goffman
by Jessica Shi

Sherri Goffman
Director of Elementary Education
Mineola Union Free School District

From Mrs. Patricia B. Molloy, The Principal

What better way to learn than by writing, illustrating, and editing a book?

The Gizmo Tales: Working Dogs brought Meadow Drive School and our community together. Students learned language arts skills while viewing dogs from a completely different perspective. Neighbors visited Meadow with responsible, intelligent and life-saving animals. Computer technology afforded the freedom to communicate with people around the world.

Our students observed how people with serious health issues and disabilities lead full, productive lives. They learned that people must communicate and respect one another's ideas for every voice to be heard. Students have come to recognize and utilize the talents of their peers.

Mrs. Molloy
by Brad Carlin

I want to thank and commend everyone on their expertise and dedication. Congratulations to our brilliantly talented 5th grade authors. We wouldn't have *Gizmo Tales: Working Dogs* without you!

From The 5th Grade Teachers

Watching the writing process come alive each week was truly rewarding. The children listened, questioned, and discovered various dogs and their special handlers. Students developed interviewing skills. Natural curiosity sparked imagination and creativity in writing *The Gizmo Tales: Working Dogs*.

Ms. Collis, our art teacher, helped the students create very professional potraits. Mrs. Parendo and Mrs. Teemsma helped make e-mail correspondence possible. Our school nurse, Mrs. Sieber, explained the medical aspects of our project. Thank you, Dr. Fink and Mrs. Paltrowitz, our authors, and our Principal Mrs. Molloy, for your support.

Mrs. Van Bell
by Elena Portillo

Mr. Tramonte
by Carly Rome

Mrs. Beyrer
by Michelle Chin

Thanks To The Educational Specialists!

**Ms. Collis,
Art Teacher**
by
Michelle Chin

**Ms. Nelson,
School Librarian**
by
Alexandria Sais

**Mrs. Parendo,
Computer Teacher**
by
Melissa D'Esposito

**Mrs. Sieber,
School Nurse**
by
Angelica Campagnoli

Thanks For Your Support!

Mrs. Hale
by
Robert Steinmann

Mrs. Karlewicz
by
Elena Portillo

Mrs. Kasny
by
Alexandria Sais

Mrs. Teemsma
by
Alexandra D'Esposito

Thanks To The Meadow Drive PTA!

Illustration by Kelly Ng

Meadow Drive PTA Officers

President: Laurie Stavish
Vice President: Denise Collins
2nd VP: Pat Molloy
3rd VP: Connie Killian
Treasurer: MaryEllen Steinmann
Recording Secretary: Teresa Barron
Corresponding Secretary: Peggy Gorry
Historian: Irene Small

Thanks To The Board of Education!

Illustration by Alyssa Trivigno

Board of Education Members

Board President: Stephen Siwinski
Vice President: RoseAnn Buglione
Trustee: John McGrath
Trustee: Donna Strein
Trustee: Mary Ellen Williams

Meet Jeri Fink and Donna Paltrowitz

Dr. Jeri Fink
by Michelle Chin

Mrs. Paltrowitz
by Philip Wacker

Jeri Fink and Donna Paltrowitz are long-time friends and colleagues, who have collaborated on many projects. They believe that young people should be active participants in the reading and writing of their own literature. Together, they developed many series, including *Books By Kids, Books By Teens, You Are The Author!, Be Part of The Story,* and *The Gizmo Tales.*

Dr. Fink is a Family Therapist, journalist, and author of books for children and adults. Donna is an educator who has co-authored more than sixty children's books and software programs. They are neighbors in Bellmore, New York, living with their respective families, cats, and of course, Gizmo.

Read All The Gizmo Books!

Corey's Web Unleashed
Corey's Web: Down In The Dumps
Matthew's Tangled Trails

Check Out Corey and Gizmo's friends (for upper elementary and middle school readers):

Matthew's Web
Who Stole Matthew's Web?
Matthew's Tangled Trails
Matthew's Web Unplugged

Visit us online to order books or to check out our workshops and educational programs:

www.bookwebpublishing.com

or contact:
Book Web Publishing, Ltd.
PO Box 81
Bellmore, NY 11710